Blackbeard

STARTER LEVEL 250 HEADWORDS

Great Clarendon Street, Oxford OX2 6DP

Oxford University Press is a department of the University of Oxford.
It furthers the University's objective of excellence in research, scholarship, and education by publishing worldwide in

Oxford New York

Auckland Cape Town Dar es Salaam Hong Kong Karachi
Kuala Lumpur Madrid Melbourne Mexico City Nairobi
New Delhi Shanghai Taipei Toronto

With offices in

Argentina Austria Brazil Chile Czech Republic France Greece
Guatemala Hungary Italy Japan Poland Portugal Singapore
South Korea Switzerland Thailand Turkey Ukraine Vietnam

OXFORD and OXFORD ENGLISH are registered trade marks of
Oxford University Press in the UK and in certain other countries

First published in Dominoes 2008

2020

18

ISBN: 978 0 19 424714 6 Book
ISBN: 978 0 19 463924 8 Book and Audio Pack

Printed in China

This book is printed on paper from certified and well-managed sources.

ACKNOWLEDGEMENTS

Illustrations by: Sebastian Camagajevac/Beehive Illustration

The publisher would like to thank the following for permission to reproduce photographs: : Alamy Images ppiv (pistol/Eye Risk), 25 (sea battle/North Wind Picture Archives), 39 (Henry Morgan/Mary Evans Picture Library), 39 (female pirates/Archie Miles); iStockphoto ppiv (pirate/Mehmet Selim Aksan), iv (sword/Dave White); Mary Evans Picture Library ppiv (Alexander Spotswood, Governor of Virginia 1710-1723), 39 (Khayr Ad-Din); Shutterstock ppiv (treasure chest/James Steidl), iv (sailing ship/RCPPhoto), 13 (pirate flag/ktsdesign).

DOMINOES

Series Editors: Bill Bowler and Sue Parminter

Blackbeard

Retold by John Escott

Illustrated by Sebastian Camagajevac

John Escott has written many books for readers of all ages, and particularly enjoys writing crime and mystery thrillers. He was born in the west of England, but now lives on the south coast. When he is not writing, he visits second-hand bookshops, watches videos of old Hollywood movies, and takes long walks along empty beaches. He has also written *The Wild West*, *A Pretty Face*, *Kidnap!* and *The Big Story*, and retold *William Tell and Other Stories* for Dominoes.

ACTIVITIES

BEFORE READING

1 Match the words with the pictures. Use a dictionary to help you.

governor pirate pistol ship sword treasure

2 Complete the sentences with the things from 1 in the correct form.

a Blackbeard is a Caribbean ....

b He takes more than forty.................. from different countries in the Caribbean Sea.

c The.................. of North Carolina is Blackbeard's friend; the .... of Virginia wants to kill Blackbeard.

d Blackbeard dies when he is under forty with a .... and .... in his hands.

e He doesn't leave lots of .... behind him when he dies.

3 Compare your ideas with a partner.

Chapter 1

The year is 1717. It is a bad time to be the **captain** of a **ship** in the Caribbean. Why? Because **pirates** are **attacking** any ship on the sea, and any small town near the sea, too.

The most **famous** pirate of them all is Blackbeard. He **captures** more than forty ships in under three years. This is his story . . . .

captain the most important person on a ship

ship you use a ship to go across the water

pirate someone who takes ships and the things on them without asking

attack to begin fighting

famous that everybody knows

capture to take and not give away

When **Queen** Anne's **War** finishes in 1713, English **sailor** Edward Teach has no work. Teach is 34 years old, and comes from Bristol. He is only happy when he is at sea.

Soon Teach meets Benjamin Hornigold. Hornigold is the captain of the pirate ship the *Mary Anne*. He is one of the nicer Caribbean pirates. There is a story about him.

One day, Hornigold's **crew** go **aboard** a ship. Do they take money? No. They take the sailors' hats! Why? Because when Hornigold's crew drink a lot, they **throw** their hats into the sea!

queen the most important woman in a country

war fighting between countries or people

sailor a man who works on a ship

crew all the people who work on a ship

aboard on or onto a ship

throw to make something move from your hand through the air

Edward Teach is soon the captain of one of Hornigold's smaller ships. He is a quick thinker, and a good sailor, and he quickly learns to be a pirate.

In early 1717, Teach and Hornigold attack and capture six more small ships. The *Betty* is one of them.

One day, the **lookout** on the *Mary Anne* calls out, 'Ship to **starboard**!' The lookout is the man up on the ship's **mast**. 'It's a French ship, *La Concorde*,' he cries. *La Concorde* is a very big ship.

'Make the **guns** ready!' Captain Hornigold calls to his crew.

lookout a sailor who looks to see what is in front of the ship

starboard the right of a ship

mast the tall thing on an old ship which has the sails on it, and where a lookout sits

gun a ship can fight with this

Hornigold's three ships attack the French ship with their guns. Suddenly one of *La Concorde*'s masts comes down noisily. Some of the French crew die.

'Make ready to go aboard!' Teach tells his men.

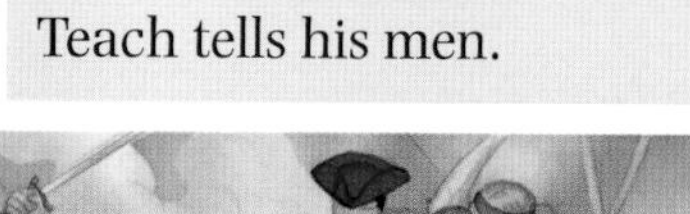

Teach and his men go aboard the French ship and the **fight** begins. Pirates and Frenchmen die, but Teach's men take the ship. The captain and crew of *La Concorde* cannot stop them.

All the *La Concorde* crew feel very afraid.
Their captain – **Pierre Dosset** – asks Teach, 'Do you want to kill us?'
'No, I don't,' Teach says. 'But tell me something. Where's all your **gold**?'
The captain does not answer.

fight when you hit someone many times

Pierre Dosset /pjeə 'dɒseɪ/

gold an expensive yellow metal

'Speak, man, or you die!' Teach says. He hits the French captain across the mouth.
'Never!' says the captain. 'Do your worst!'

Teach walks across to a young French boy. 'You, boy!' he says to him. 'What's your name?'
'**Louis Arot**, **sir**,' the boy answers.
'Where's the gold, boy?' Teach asks. 'Take me to it!'

Louis takes Teach to the captain's **cabin**.
'The gold's here, sir,' he says.
'Thank you, boy,' Teach says, and he smiles.

Louis Arot /'lu:wi 'ærəʊ/

sir you say this when you talk to an important man

cabin a room on a ship

READING CHECK

Match the people in Chapter 1 with the sentences.

Hornigold

Louis Arot

Queen Anne

Teach

the French captain

the *Mary Anne's* lookout

a ..Queen Anne.. of England dies in 1714.

b .... 's ship is the *Mary Anne*.

c One day .... and his men go on to a ship and take people's hats.

d .... comes from Bristol and works with ....

e .... sees the French ship *La Concorde* first.

f .... and his men take *La Concorde*.

g .... wants *La Concorde*'s gold, and he hits ....

h The cabin boy .... takes .... to the gold.

WORD WORK

1 Find words from Chapter 1 to match the pictures.

a 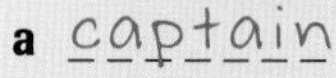 captain

b _ _ _ _

c _ _ _ _ _

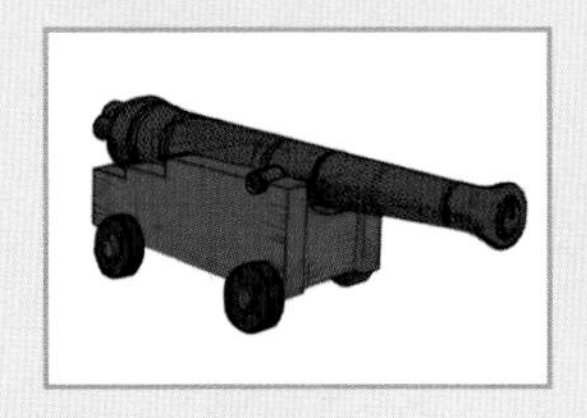

d _ _ _ _

e _ _ _

f _ _ _ _ _ _

2 Use the words in the Caribbean Sea to complete the sentences.

fight
famous
war
aboard
attack
starboard
captures
crew

a Long John Silver is a ...famous... pirate with one leg. He comes from a book by Robert Louis Stevenson.

b Queen Anne's .... is between France and England in North America. It begins in 1702 and finishes in 1713.

c Sailors, when they are looking to the front of a ship, call the right of the ship '..................'.

d There is a .... of fifty-nine Frenchmen on *La Concorde*.

e The .... between Teach's 250 pirates and the French finishes quickly.

f When Teach goes .... *La Concorde*, he meets its captain, Pierre Dosset.

g In the 1700s pirates .... many ships in the Caribbean.

h Teach .... more than forty ships in only a few years.

GUESS WHAT

What happens in the next chapter? Tick two boxes to finish each sentence.

a Edward Teach . . .

1 ☐ gives a new name to *La Concorde*.
2 ☐ leaves most of *La Concorde*'s crew alive.
3 ☐ kills all of *La Concorde*'s crew.

b Captain Pierre Dosset . . .

1 ☐ leaves *La Concorde*.
2 ☐ dies.
3 ☐ has Teach's old ship.

c Louis Arot . . .

1 ☐ goes with Teach.
2 ☐ kills Captain Dosset.
3 ☐ is now a pirate.

d Benjamin Hornigold . . .

1 ☐ dies suddenly.
2 ☐ stops being a pirate.
3 ☐ gives a ship to Teach.

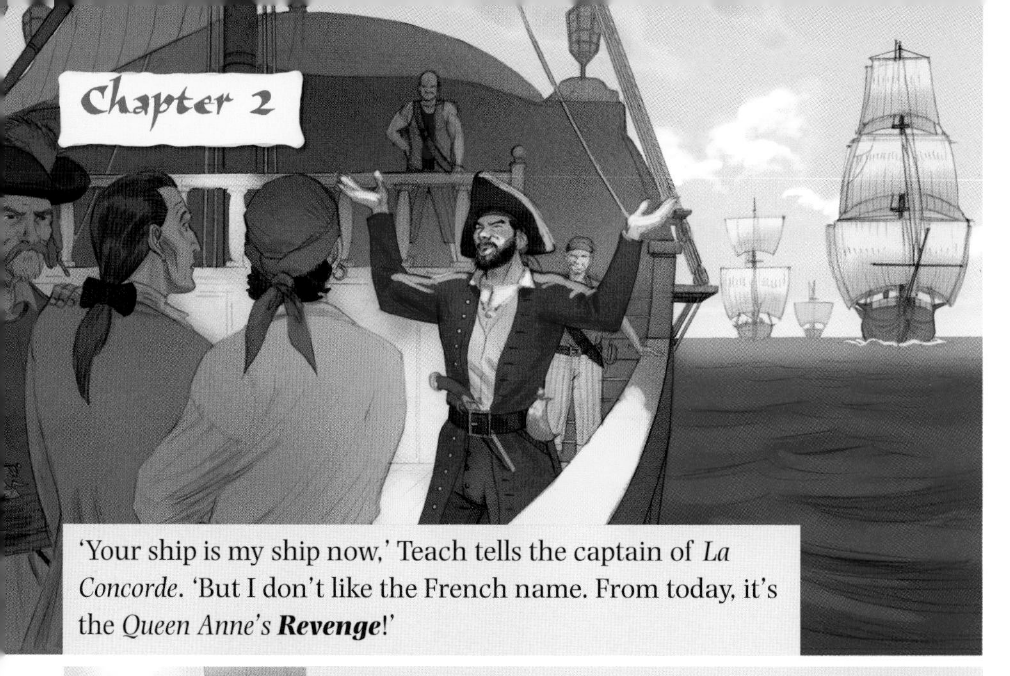

'Your ship is my ship now,' Teach tells the captain of *La Concorde*. 'But I don't like the French name. From today, it's the *Queen Anne's* **Revenge**!'

'Where are you taking us?' the French captain asks. 'To the **island** of Bequia,' Teach tells him. 'You and your crew can go **ashore** there. But perhaps some of your men want to stay aboard and go with me.'

Teach is right. Some of the Frenchmen **sail** with him. Louis Arot is one of them. 'You can have my old ship!' Teach tells the French captain.

revenge when you do something bad to someone after they do something bad to you

island a country in the sea

ashore on or onto the land

sail to go across the water

wife a woman living with a man

adventure something very exciting that happens to you

aye a sailor's 'yes'

terror a feeling of being afraid

Because Teach has a long black **beard**, people give him a new name – 'Blackbeard the Pirate'. He's the most **frightening** of all the pirates on the sea.

Alexander Spotswood is the **Governor** of Virginia. Every day, ships' captains come to him with frightening stories about Blackbeard the Pirate.

'We must stop this man Blackbeard!' Spotswood says, angrily. 'That's easy to say,' **Lieutenant** Robert Maynard of the **Royal Navy** tells him. 'But his ship, the *Queen Anne's Revenge*, is fast and it has forty guns.'

beard the hair on a man's face

frightening making people afraid

governor a person who looks after a far country for a king or queen

lieutenant /lef'tenənt/ an officer on a ship

royal navy all the king's or queen's ships

At the same time Blackbeard and his men are all ashore. They are drinking happily in the pirate town of Port Royal in Jamaica.

'Do I want to stop being a pirate, go ashore, take a wife, and live to be an old man?' thinks Blackbeard. He has fourteen wives, or a woman in every town in the Caribbean, people say.

But he cannot forget the easy money, the gold, and all of his exciting adventures at sea. And he cannot leave his pirate ship for a house ashore.

READING CHECK

Choose the correct pictures.

a Where does Teach take the crew of *La Concorde*?

1 ☑ to a small island. **2** ☐ to the city of Port Royal. **3** ☐ to the Governor of Virginia.

b What does Teach give to the French captain?

1 ☐ gold. **2** ☐ a small island. **3** ☐ his old ship.

c Who does Louis Arot go with?

1 ☐ Hornigold. **2** ☐ Teach. **3** ☐ the French captain Pierre Dosset.

d Who does Hornigold go home to?

1 ☐ his wife. **2** ☐ his young son. **3** ☐ his old mother.

WORD WORK

Use the words in the pirate flag to complete the sentences.

a Teach gets his name 'Blackbeard the Pirate' from his long black . beard . .

b Jamaica is an ....

c Mary Ormond was Blackbeard's .... number fourteen.

d Sailors don't say 'yes', they say say '................'.

e Blackbeard is a .... man, and many ships' captains are afraid of him.

f Bill Clinton was the .... of Arkansas for many years.

g Blackbeard has many exciting .... before he dies.

h The .... is the name for all the king's or queen's ships and sailors.

i Blackbeard the Pirate .... the Caribbean for five years – from 1713 to 1718.

j A .... is an officer on a ship. He is not as important as a captain.

k Blackbeard's name brings .... to people's faces when they hear it.

l When sailors leave their ships to visit islands, they 'go ....' .

m When you kill people in my family, I kill people in your family. That's ....

GUESS WHAT

What does Blackbeard do in the next chapter? Tick three sentences.

a ☐ He captures a Spanish ship.

b ☐ He meets Governor Spotswood.

c ☐ He leaves some Spanish sailors on a small island.

d ☐ He has a fight with Lieutenant Maynard.

e ☐ He attacks the town of Charleston.

f ☐ He talks about finding help for his crew when they are ill.

Chapter 3
In April that year, Blackbeard captures a new ship – the *Adventure* – near Honduras. 'You can sail with me, Herriot,' he tells the captain. 'You can be one of my crew.'
Captain David Herriot is afraid. He cannot say 'no' to Blackbeard. 'Aye, aye, Captain,' he says.
Some weeks later, they sail near the Cayman Islands.

'Spanish ship to starboard, captain!' calls the lookout of the *Queen Anne's Revenge*.

'To the guns men!' Blackbeard calls. 'And be ready to go aboard when I say!'
The guns of the *Queen Anne's Revenge* and the *Adventure* are soon **firing** at the Spanish ship.

'To the **boats**!' Blackbeard tells his men. The men put **small** boats into the sea and **jump** into them.

fire to attack with a gun

boat a little ship

small little

jump to move fast on your legs from one thing to a different thing

When Blackbeard and his men go aboard the Spanish ship, the Spanish crew and their captain are ready and waiting. And they fight well.

But Blackbeard has many men, and in the end he captures the ship. With his long black beard, his **pistols**, and his **sword** he looks a very frightening man.

Soon after that, Blackbeard puts the captain and the crew of the Spanish ship ashore on a small island. Now the ***Cubana*** is Blackbeard's ship, too.

pistol a person can kill someone with this

sword a long knife that you fight with

Cubana /kuː'bænæ/

In May 1718 Blackbeard and his ships are near the town of Charleston in South Carolina.

'We need **medicine**,' the ship's **doctor** tells Blackbeard. 'Some of the crew have a **fever**, and there's no medicine for them on the ship.'
'Then let's find some,' Blackbeard says.

'How?' the doctor asks. 'We can't go into Charleston. We're pirates, and they can capture us and kill us there.'
'Then the good people of Charleston can bring the medicine to us,' Blackbeard says, and he laughs.

medicine something that you eat or drink to help you get better when you are ill

doctor a person who helps people when they are ill

fever when you get very hot because you are ill

ACTIVITIES

READING CHECK

Are these sentences true or false? Tick the boxes.

		True	False
a	Blackbeard captures the ship *The Adventure* near Honduras.	☑	☐
b	He tells the captain, David Herriot, 'You must die.'	☐	☐
c	He captures a Spanish ship near the Cayman Islands.	☐	☐
d	The Spanish crew and their captain fight badly.	☐	☐
e	Blackbeard kills the Spanish captain and his crew.	☐	☐
f	Many of Blackbeard's crew are ill when his ships are near Charleston, South Carolina.	☐	☐
g	Blackbeard's pirates can easily go into Charleston for help.	☐	☐

WORD WORK

Correct the sentences about the pictures with words from Chapter 3.

a There are a lot of goats in the sea.

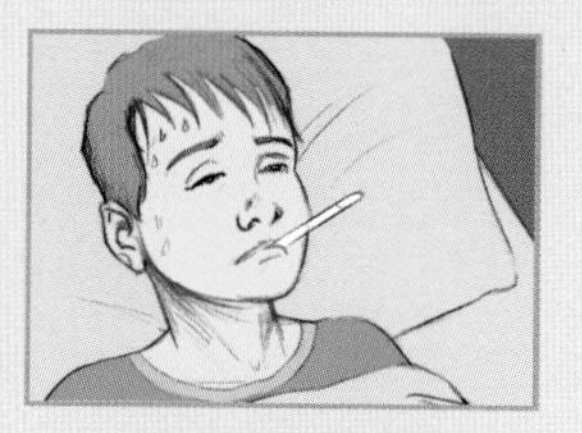

b He's got a bad lever.

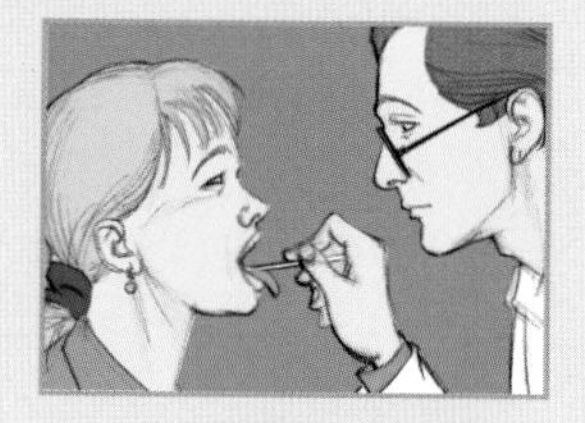

c Her daughter looked at her carefully.

d When you feel tired, this magazine can help you.

e Be careful when you are tiring your gun not to hit someone.

f Do you want the big apple or the smell apple?

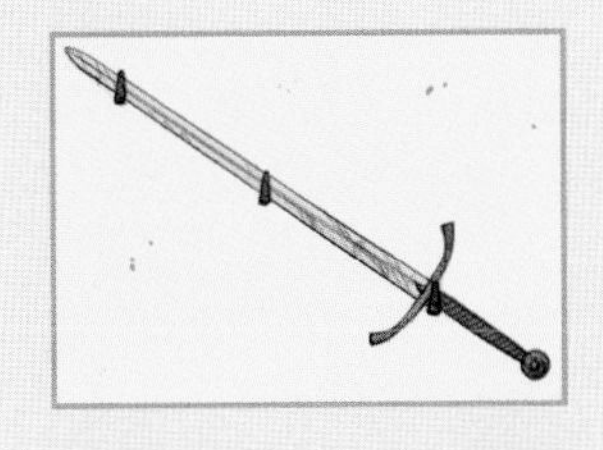

g I can bump from this chair to that chair.

h That's a very old chord.

i In the old days people had piston fights.

GUESS WHAT

What happens in the next chapter? Tick two boxes.

a ☐ Blackbeard stops all ships going into Charleston.
b ☐ A Royal Navy ship captures Blackbeard's ship.
c ☐ Blackbeard fights Lieutenant Maynard.
d ☐ Medicine comes for Blackbeard's crew from the Governor of South Carolina.

There is a Charleston **councillor** aboard the *Crowley*. His young son is with him. The boy is four years old, and there is terror in his eyes.
'I want to go ashore now,' the councillor tells Blackbeard.
'Do you?' Blackbeard says. He smiles. 'Perhaps in a day or two. But first you can write a **letter** to the Governor of South Carolina.'

surrender to stop fighting because you cannot win

councillor an important man that looks after a town

letter you write this to tell something to someone

'A letter?' the councillor says. 'What do I write?'
'Tell the governor, "**Send** a **chest** of medicine to the *Queen Anne's Revenge*",' Blackbeard says. 'You and your son can go to Charleston when the medicine arrives, but not before then.'

'Tell the governor, "No ships can come into – or leave – Charleston before the medicine arrives on the *Queen Anne's Revenge*,"' Blackbeard says.

When it is ready, two of Blackbeard's men take the letter to the governor.

send to give something to someone to take somewhere **chest** a big box to put things in

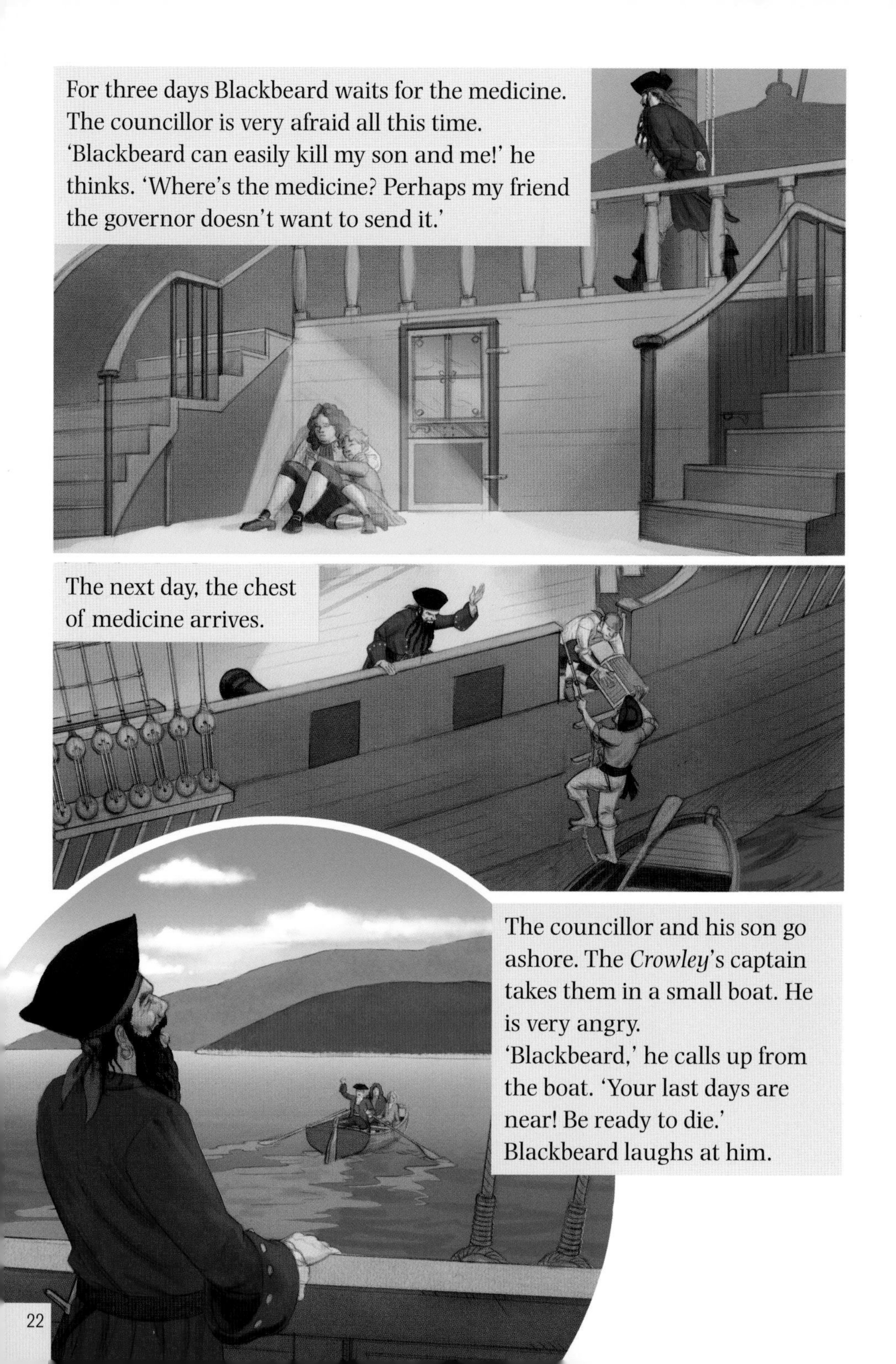
For three days Blackbeard waits for the medicine. The councillor is very afraid all this time. 'Blackbeard can easily kill my son and me!' he thinks. 'Where's the medicine? Perhaps my friend the governor doesn't want to send it.'
The next day, the chest of medicine arrives.
The councillor and his son go ashore. The *Crowley*'s captain takes them in a small boat. He is very angry.
'Blackbeard,' he calls up from the boat. 'Your last days are near! Be ready to die.'
Blackbeard laughs at him.

Later that year, Blackbeard gives Charles Eden some gold. Eden is the Governor of North Carolina. He gives a **pardon** from **King** George to his friend Blackbeard.

The next day, Blackbeard captures a French ship and kills its crew. He gives **sugar** from the ship to Eden.
'No more pirate adventures, Blackbeard. Don't forget your pardon,' says Eden.

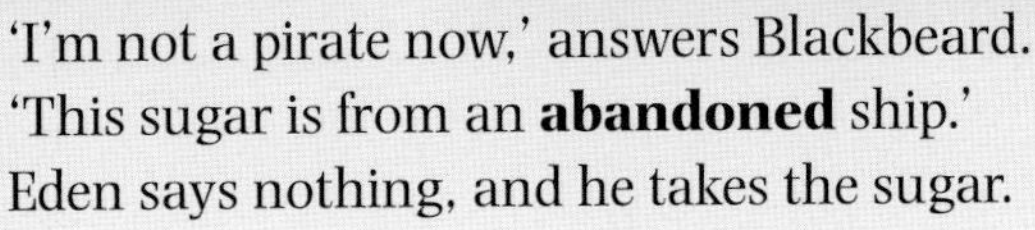

'I'm not a pirate now,' answers Blackbeard. 'This sugar is from an **abandoned** ship.' Eden says nothing, and he takes the sugar.

pardon a letter from someone important which says that someone bad does not need to die

king the most important man in a country

sugar this is white or brown and sweet

abandoned with no men on it

READING CHECK

Choose the correct words to complete these sentences.

a Blackbeard captures eight more ships / towns .

b On the *Crowley* he finds an important man from London / Charleston and his young son.

c The man writes a letter to the Governor of South Carolina / King of England .

d The letter asks for medicine / gold for Blackbeard.

e Blackbeard stops ships going into Charleston / Port Royal and waits for an answer to the letter.

f Three days / weeks later the answer arrives.

g When the answer comes, Blackbeard is happy / angry .

h In the end, the important man and his son die / go home .

i The Governor of North / South Carolina is Blackbeard's friend.

j Blackbeard gets a pardon from King George / Queen Anne .

WORD WORK

Complete the sentences with the words in the pirate swords.

a A town c o u n c i l l o r works to make things better for the people in a town.

b Stop your fight with us, and _ _ _ _ _ _ _ _ _. My crew is bigger than your crew.

c In the captain's cabin there's a big _ _ _ _ _ with gold in it.

d There's an old car by the road with no one in it. It's an _ _ _ _ _ _ _ _ _ car.

e Do you want some _ _ _ _ _ in your hot milk?

clonocirlu

rurneserd

shect

debondana

argus

f We're _ _ _ _ _ _ _ _ you some money. You can get something nice with it.

g The king is giving you a _ _ _ _ _ _. No one can capture you and kill you in his name now. So you can stop being a pirate and be a good man.

h I'm writing a _ _ _ _ _ _ to my aunt to say 'thank you' for the book.

GUESS WHAT

What happens in the next chapter? Tick the boxes.

		Yes	No
a	Governor Spotswood hears about Blackbeard's adventures in Boston.	☐	☐
b	He sends Lieutenant Maynard after Blackbeard.	☐	☐
c	Maynard dies in a fight with Blackbeard.	☐	☐
d	Blackbeard leaves two of his bigger ships and their crews behind.	☐	☐
e	He takes all his gold with him in a smaller ship.	☐	☐
f	Blackbeard's men kill him before the Royal Navy can capture him.	☐	☐

The Virginia Governor, Alexander Spotswood, hears the **news** about Blackbeard's **blockade** of Charleston. 'He can't do this to us!' Spotswood says, angrily.

Lieutenant Robert Maynard of the British Royal Navy is with the governor.
'How can we catch Blackbeard?' Spotswood asks him.
'He isn't an easy man to find,' Maynard says. 'We need help. We must wait for more ships from England.'
'No,' Spotswood says. 'We must do something *now*.'

Soon after that, Blackbeard sails to Old **Topsail Inlet** in North Carolina. By now, there are three hundred pirates on his three ships.

When they arrive, the *Queen Anne's Revenge* and one of the smaller ships – the *Cubana* – go **aground**. Only the *Adventure* is all right because she is far behind them.

news when someone tells you something new

blockade when someone stops ships arriving at or leaving a town by the sea

topsail this sail goes up near the top of the mast

inlet a small arm of the sea that has land to left and right

aground on land that is not under much water, from which it is difficult for a ship to move

'We must wait for the sea to come in tonight before we can move,' Blackbeard tells his crew. 'Take some **rum** ashore in the small boats, and wait there.'
So the pirates from the *Queen Anne's Revenge* and the *Cubana* make their boats ready to go ashore.

When the boats are ashore, Blackbeard speaks quietly with some of the pirates.

That evening, Blackbeard's men drink rum and sing. Most of them drink a lot, and they go to sleep early before it's dark.

rum an alcoholic drink made from sugar

But some don't drink much, and they don't go to sleep. 'Come with me,' Blackbeard says quietly to these men. 'We can go now.'

They take three of the small boats out to the *Adventure*. And they take all of the **treasure** with them, too.

In the morning, the pirates ashore look for the *Adventure*. 'Where's the ship?' they ask. 'More importantly, where's Blackbeard?'
'And most important of all, where's the treasure?' cries one man.

treasure something expensive, like gold

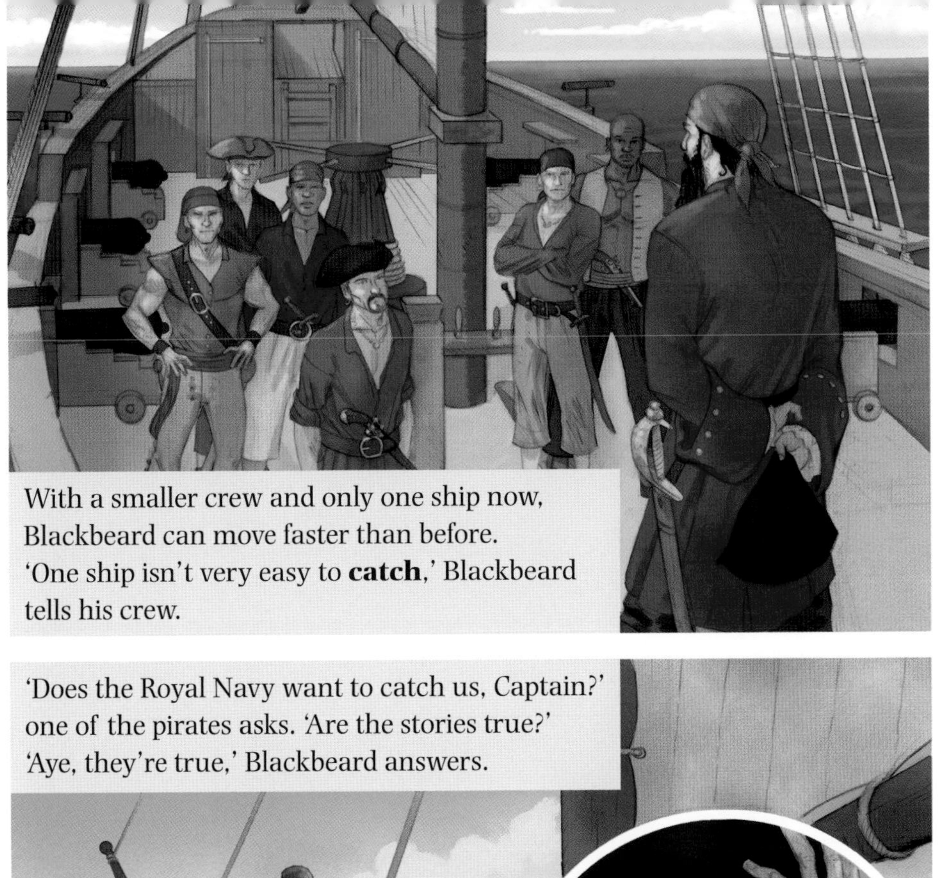

catch to take quickly

ACTIVITIES

READING CHECK

Correct the sentences.

a Alexander Spotswood is happy when he hears about Blackbeard's Charleston adventure.

b Blackbeard sails his four ships to North Carolina.

c Three of his ships go aground there.

d The pirates must wait for the sea to go out before they can move these ships.

e They go ashore in big boats.

f Many of Blackbeard's men drink and go to sleep late that night.

g Blackbeard and some of his men take boats out to the *Queen Anne's Revenge*.

h They take all Blackbeard's rum with them too.

i The Governor of North Carolina wants Blackbeard dead.

WORD WORK

1 Read the sentences and complete the puzzle with words from Chapter 5.

a Spotswood wants to . . . Blackbeard and kill him.
b There's a . . . of the airport. No planes can arrive or leave.
c What's the latest . . . about the war?
d Be careful with the boat! The sea is out now. We don't want to go . . . .
e There's a little . . . on the island and small ships can stop there.
f On the island of Monte Cristo there's a big chest with . . . in it.
g . . . is a drink from the Caribbean.

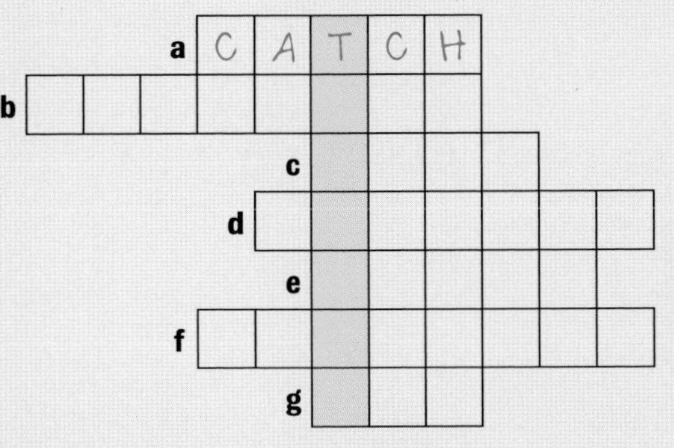

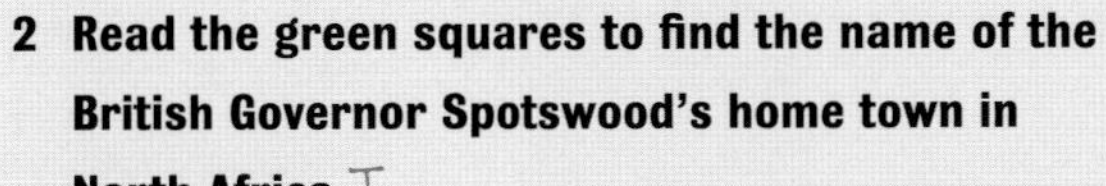

2 Read the green squares to find the name of the British Governor Spotswood's home town in North Africa. T _ _ _ _ _ _

GUESS WHAT

How does the story end? Tick one box.

- **a** ☐ Blackbeard dies slowly in front of Spotswood.
- **b** ☐ Blackbeard dies suddenly in a fight.
- **c** ☐ Blackbeard dies happily in bed when he is very old.
- **d** ☐ Nobody knows when Blackbeard dies.

Chapter 6

In December 1718, Governor Spotswood hears more news about Blackbeard. 'He's at Ocracoke Inlet near North Carolina,' a Royal Navy captain tells him. 'Do you hear that, Maynard?' Spotswood asks. 'What can we do about it?'

'I can take the *Jane* up to North Carolina with 35 men aboard,' Maynard says. 'And the *Ranger* can come with us, with 25 men under their captain, Mr Hyde.'

'Good,' Spotswood says. 'When can you leave?' 'In two days,' Maynard answers. Spotswood laughs. 'Blackbeard, we've got you!' he says.

On December 21, 1718 the ships *Jane* and *Ranger* sail to Ocracoke Inlet. They put down their **anchors**.

Some of Blackbeard's crew are in the town of Bath not far away. Only eighteen men are with him on his ship, the *Adventure*.

'The Royal Navy's here, Captain!' the lookout calls.
'They're waiting for morning before they attack,' Blackbeard says.

Blackbeard drinks some rum.
'Can this be my last night, and my last fight tomorrow?' he thinks.

anchor a heavy metal thing that a ship puts down into the water when it wants to stop somewhere

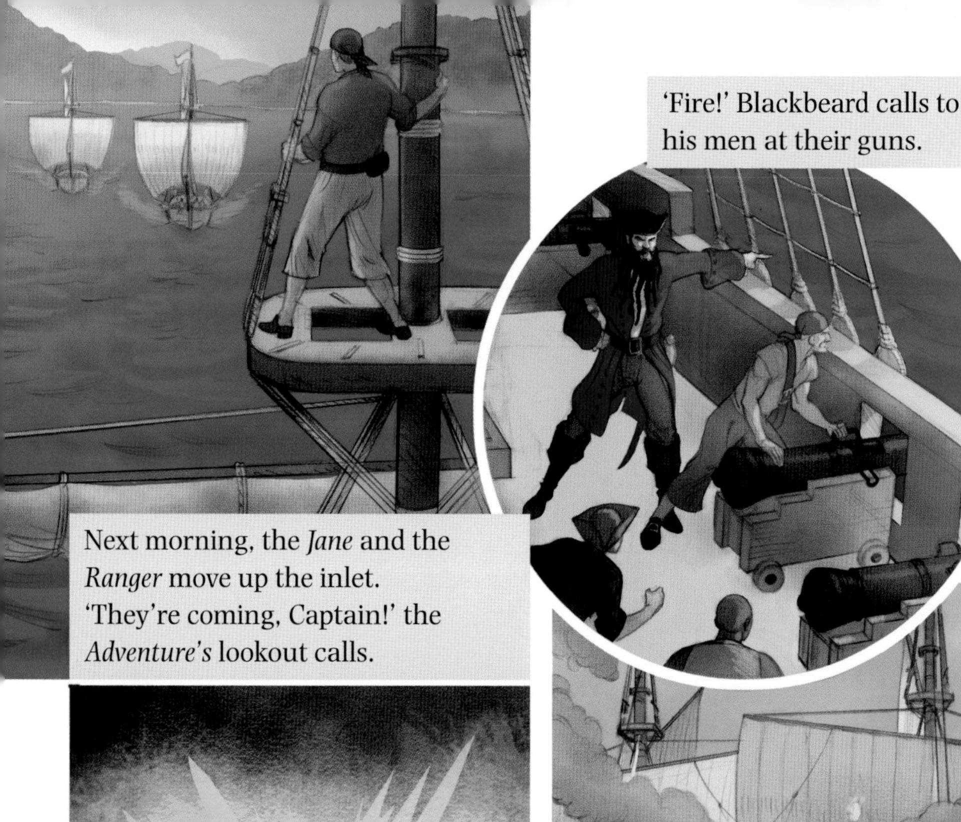

Next morning, the *Jane* and the *Ranger* move up the inlet. 'They're coming, Captain!' the *Adventure's* lookout calls.

'Fire!' Blackbeard calls to his men at their guns.

The *Adventure*'s guns hit the *Ranger* and kill some sailors. Captain Hyde, is one of them.

Lieutenant Maynard brings the *Jane* next to the *Adventure*. 'Guns ready!' Maynard calls to his gunners. 'Fire!'

'Look! There aren't many sailors on **deck** there now!' Blackbeard calls to his men. 'Let's fight them!' And he jumps across to the *Jane*.

But Maynard's men are waiting. Suddenly they all come out from **below** the deck and begin to fight the pirates.

Now Blackbeard meets Maynard. 'Are you ready to die, Lieutenant?' Blackbeard asks, and he laughs. Maynard does not answer, but he hits Blackbeard's arm with his sword.

One of the sailors fires his pistol at Blackbeard.

deck where you walk on a ship

below under

Project A A Wanted Poster

1 Complete the Wanted Poster for 'Blackbeard' with the words and phrases from the box.

38	beard	long, black	'Blackbeard'	blockading	Bristol, England
the Caribbean	Edward Teach, Tatch, or Thatch		Governor Spotswood		pistols
Queen Anne's Revenge	40 ships	tall, frightening	treasure	14 wives	

WANTED DEAD OR ALIVE

Reward of 500 gold doubloons for the capture of the Pirate ______________________

Real Name: ______________________

Age: ______________________

From: ______________________

Lives in: ______________________,

on his ship the ______________________

Crimes: capturing more than ____________, ______________________ stealing lots of ______________________, ____________ Charleston, marrying ____________

Appearance: a ______________________ man with a ______________________ beard, usually wears lots of ______________________ in his belt and puts smoking fireworks in his ______________________

Contact: ______________________ of Virginia

2 **Make a Wanted Poster for the pirate 'Mary Read' with the information in these notes.**

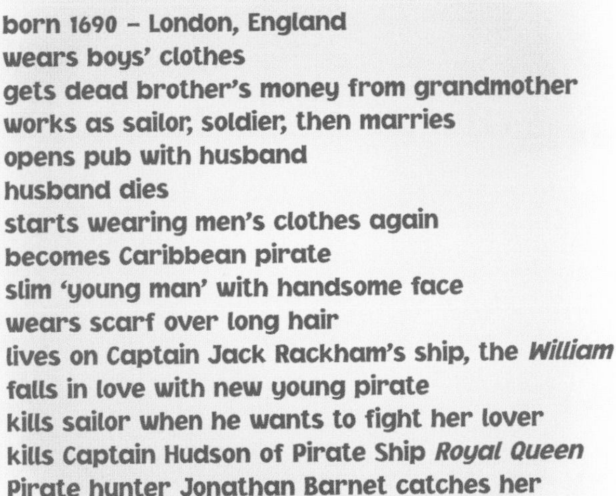

Mary Read

born 1690 – London, England
wears boys' clothes
gets dead brother's money from grandmother
works as sailor, soldier, then marries
opens pub with husband
husband dies
starts wearing men's clothes again
becomes Caribbean pirate
slim 'young man' with handsome face
wears scarf over long hair
lives on Captain Jack Rackham's ship, the *William*
falls in love with new young pirate
kills sailor when he wants to fight her lover
kills Captain Hudson of Pirate Ship *Royal Queen*
Pirate hunter Jonathan Barnet catches her
dies in 1721 in prison having Jack Rackham's child

3 **Choose a different real life pirate and find out more about him or her. Imagine your pirate is alive today. Complete these sentences about him or her.**

a His/Her nickname is . . .
b His/Her real name is . . .
c He/She is from . . .
d He/She lives in . . .
e His/Her crimes are . . .
f He/She looks . . .
g He/She usually wears . . .
h . . . is looking for him/her.
i He/She is . . . years old when he/she dies.

4 **Make a Wanted Poster for your pirate with the information in 3.**

Project B A Pirate Treasure Map

1 Look at Blackbeard's map on page 43. Complete his instructions below.

Instructions to Find My Treasure

Sail your ship past Springer's __________ in the south-west of Ocracoke Island, and put down your anchor in Teach's Channel near The Ditch.

Leave your ship and go in a boat into Silver Lake __________ .

Leave your boat near Pilot __________ , and walk north-east through Widgeon __________ to Oyster Creek __________ .

Go south-east across the river and walk past the Old __________ on your right with Horsepen Point on your left.

When you come to Hammock __________ , walk south-east over them. Then turn right and walk south-west along Shipwreck __________ . When the fourth __________ is on your right, stop.

The treasure chest is under your feet.

2 Read the completed instructions in 1. Mark your moves on the above map with a dotted line (– – – –). Put an X where the treasure is.

3 Make a Pirate Treasure Map. Draw an island, name it, and put these things on it. Give them interesting pirate names.

bay	hill	inlet	river	rock	swamp	village/town	wood/forest

4 Imagine there is a treasure chest on your island. Write instructions to find it.

5 Work in pairs. Swap maps and instructions. Read your partner's instructions. Mark your moves on their map with a dotted line (– – – –). Put an X where the treasure is.

6 Check your partner's work. Are they right?

Treasure Map

Instructions

GRAMMAR CHECK

Present Continuous: Yes/No questions and short answers

We form questions in the Present Continuous with is or are and the –ing form of the verb. For short answers, we reuse the auxiliary verb. The pronoun in the short answer matches the noun or pronoun in the question.

Is it raining? — *No, it isn't. (is not)*

Are the children playing? — *Yes, they are.*

1 Look at the picture and write short answers to the questions.

a Is the young woman looking at Blackbeard? No, she isn't.

b Is Blackbeard looking at the woman? ....

c Is the woman wearing a blue dress? ....

d Is she taking some drinks to the men? ....

e Are the men drinking?..........................

f Are the men sleeping? ....

g Is the man on the right smiling? ....

h Is the smoke under the table? ....

2 Now look at the picture and complete the text with the Present Continuous form of the verbs in the box.

walk	~~fight~~	not eat	smoke	talk
sit	take	look	drink	stand

Blackbeard and his men are all ashore. Are they a) fighting? No, they b) .... at a table and they c) .... something. They d) .... because they aren't hungry. A young woman e) .... to the table. She f) .... more drinks to the men. Blackbeard g) .... at her face. A man h) .... behind the table. Some people i) .... because we can see smoke in the picture. The man on the right j) .... to the man on the left.

GRAMMAR CHECK

Information questions and question words

We use question words in information questions.

Where is Blackbeard from?

Why is he famous?

When is he truly happy?

We answer these questions by giving some information.

Bristol, in England.

Because he captures a lot of ships.

When he is at sea.

3 Complete the information questions with the question words in the box.

~~Why~~	How many	What	How much	Where
When	Where	Which	Who	Why

a Q: ....Why.... is 1717 a bad time for ships in the Caribbean?
A: Because pirates are attacking any ship on the sea.

b Q: .... do Teach and Hornigold capture six ships?
A: In early 1717.

c Q: .... does the lookout see from the *Mary Anne*?
A: *La Concorde*, a French ship.

d Q: .... is the gold on *La Concorde*?
A: In the captain's cabin.

e Q: .... does Teach take *La Concorde*?
A: To the island of Bequia.

f Q: .... do people give Teach a new name?
A: Because he has a long, black beard.

g Q: .... guns are there on the *Queen Anne's Revenge*?
A: Forty.

h Q: .... governor wants to stop Blackbeard?
A: The Governor of Virginia, Alexander Spotswood.

i Q: .... treasure has Blackbeard got when he dies?
A: Nobody knows.

j Q: .... puts Blackbeard's head at the front of his ship?
A: Captain Maynard.

GRAMMAR CHECK

There is and there are

We use there is (there's) and there are to talk about the things and people in a place.

There's a big ship out at sea. *There are a lot of pirate attacks in 1717.*

To make the sentence negative, we use there is/there are + not (there isn't/there aren't).

There aren't many sailors on the island.

In questions we change the order of there and the verb is/are.

Is there a pirate on the ship? *Are there any guns?*

We don't use contractions in affirmative short answers.

Yes, there is. ✓ *Yes, there's.* ✗

4 Complete the text with *there is* or *there are*.

Blackbeard and his ships are near Charleston in South Carolina. Some of the crew have a fever and a) there is no medicine for them on the ship. Of course b) .... medicine in Charleston but the pirates can't go ashore. That week, Blackbeard captures eight ships. The *Crowley* is one of them. On the *Crowley* c) .... a lot of men. d) .... a Charleston councillor and e) .... a young boy, the councillor's son. The councillor writes a letter to the Governor of South Carolina. f) '............... any medicine for Blackbeard and his men?' he asks. After three days, the medicine arrives. g) ....a small boat on Blackbeard's ship and it takes the councillor and his son ashore. The councillor is very angry. h) '................. no pirates worse than you!' he cries, 'Be ready to die!' Blackbeard laughs at him. 'You're right!' he cries, i) '................ no pirate worse than me!'

5 Write short answers to these questions.

a Is there a lookout on the *Queen Anne's Revenge*? Yes, there is.

b Are there any women in Blackbeard's life? ....

c Is there a good governor in Virginia? ....

d Is there a German crew on *La Concorde*? ....

e Are there a lot of women pirates in the Caribbean? ....

GRAMMAR CHECK

Prepositions of movement

Prepositions of movement tell us how something moves.

up	**down**	**into**
out of	**over**	**through**
across	**past**	**to**

6 Complete the text about Blackbeard's last fight with the prepositions in the box.

across	down	into	out of	~~to~~
over	past	through	to	up

In December 1718, the ships *Jane* and *Ranger* sail a) ..to.. Ocracoke Inlet. Their anchors go b) .... into the sea. Blackbeard is on his ship, the *Adventure*, with eighteen men.

The next day, the *Jane* and *Ranger* move c) .... the inlet. The men fight. After a time, there aren't many sailors on the *Jane*. 'Let's fight them!' calls Blackbeard and he jumps d) .... to the *Jane*. Maynard's men are waiting. Suddenly, they all come e) .... a dark room below the deck. They begin to fight the pirates. Maynard fires his pistol at Blackbeard again and again. Then Maynard jumps f) .... the bodies on the deck. He runs g) .... more pirates and he puts his sword h) .... Blackbeard's body. The pirate dies and Maynard sails back i) .... Virginia with Blackbeard's head on the front of his ship.

GRAMMAR CHECK

Present Simple: affirmative

With most verbs in the Present Simple, we add –s to make the form of the verb.

Teach quickly learns to be a pirate.

He takes more than forty ships.

After the verbs *go, teach, finish*, and *watch* we add –es.

The lookout on a ship watches the sea day and night.

When verbs end in consonant + y – *bury, cry*, and *marry* – we change y into i and add –es.

Captain Hornigold marries a good woman.

The verbs *be* and *have* are irregular.

Blackbeard is rich and he has (has got) a lot of treasure.

7 Complete the text about Blackbeard's first adventures with the Present Simple form of the verbs in brackets.

When the story a) begins (begin), Blackbeard b) .... (be) 34 years old.

He c) .... (come) from Bristol and he loves the sea. One day he d) .... (meet) Captain Hornigold, the captain of the *Mary Anne*. In 1717, Blackbeard and Hornigold e) .... (capture) six small ships. Later, they see a French ship, *La Concorde*. Hornigold f) .... (cry) to his crew, 'Make the guns ready!' Blackbeard g) .... (watch) and then he h) .... (go) aboard the French ship. Blackbeard knows it i) .... (have got) lots of gold on board. He j) .... (take) the gold and he gives the ship a new name – the *Queen Anne's Revenge*. The ship sails to the island of Bequia. There, some of the men k) .... (go) ashore and some of them l) .... (stay) on board. For the next half year, Blackbeard and his crew bring terror to the Caribbean. Soon, everybody m) .... (know) about Blackbeard.

GRAMMAR CHECK

Possessive 's and s'

We use the possessive 's and s' when we want to show that something belongs to someone or something.

When the person or thing is singular, we use 's.

The ship's captain is a good man.

The pirate's beard is black.

When the person or thing is plural, we use s'.

The ships' crews are ready.

The pirates' treasure is on the island.

With irregular plural nouns, we use 's.

The children's mother is tired.

The men's jobs are interesting.

8 Rewrite the sentences using the possessive *'s or s'*.

a The War of Queen Anne finishes in 1713.

........Queen Anne's War........ finishes in 1713.

b The crew of Hornigold drink a lot.

....

c One of the masts of *La Concorde* comes down.

....

d Hornigold is tired of his adventures of a pirate.

....

e The captains of all the ships know about Blackbeard.

....

f The adventures of the men are exciting.

....

g The doctor of the ship tells Blackbeard, 'We need medicine.'

....

GRAMMAR CHECK

Linkers: and, but, so, and because

and links two parts of a sentence with the same idea.

Teach loves the sea and he loves treasure too.

but links two parts of a sentence with different ideas.

Governor Charles Eden doesn't like Blackbeard, but he takes his sugar.

so links two parts of a sentence talking about the result of something.

Spotswood and Maynard want to catch Blackbeard so they sail to Ocracoke Inlet.

(result of first part of sentence)

because links two parts of a sentence talking about the reason for something.

Blackbeard laughs because Maynard's sword breaks.

(reason for first part of sentence)

9 Complete the sentences with *and, but, so,* or *because.*

a Edward Teach is a sailor ...and... he is 34 years old.

b Teach is soon a captain .... he is a quick thinker and a good sailor.

c Teach and his men go aboard the French ship .... the fight begins.

d Teach asks the French captain, 'Where's your gold?' .... the captain doesn't answer.

e Teach takes a young boy to the captain's cabin .... he can find the gold.

f The boy doesn't want to help Teach .... he takes him to the gold .... he is afraid of him.

g Blackbeard's ship is fast .... it has forty guns.

h Teach has a long black beard .... people call him Blackbeard.

DOMINOES Your Choice

Read *Dominoes* for pleasure, or to develop language skills. It's your choice.

Each *Domino* reader includes:

- a good story to enjoy
- integrated activities to develop reading skills and increase vocabulary
- task-based projects – perfect for CEFR portfolios
- contextualized grammar activities

Each *Domino* pack contains a reader, and an excitingly dramatized audio recording of the story

If you liked this *Domino*, read these:

Hercules

Retold by Janet Hardy-Gould

Hercules is the strongest man in the world, but one day he does something very bad.

The priestess at Delphi tells him: 'The gods are angry with you. For twelve years you must work for King Eurystheus, and do twelve tasks for him. When you finish, the gods can forgive your crime.'

Some tasks are easier, and some tasks are more difficult.

Can Hercules finish all twelve of them? And what happens when he does?

The Great Fire of London

Janet Hardy-Gould

It's London, 1666. It's a hot, dry summer. A small fire starts in a baker's shop in Pudding Lane. Soon the city of London is burning and the fire-fighters can't stop the fire. People are running from their houses down to the River Thames.

But how does the fire begin and who can stop it? What is the King of England doing to help?

	CEFR	Cambridge Exams	IELTS	TOEFL iBT	TOEIC
Level 3	B1	PET	4.0	57-86	550
Level 2	A2–B1	KET-PET	3.0-4.0	–	390
Level 1	A1–A2	YLE Flyers/KET	3.0	–	225
Starter & Quick Starter	A1	YLE Movers	1.0–2.0	–	–

You can find details and a full list of books and teachers' resources on our website:
www.oup.com/elt/gradedreaders